YPS

QED

QED Publishing

D0307795

First published in the UK in 2009 by
QED Publishing
A Quarto Group company
226 City Road
London EC1V 2TT

www.qed-publishing.co.uk

A catalogue record for this book is available
from the British Library.

ISBN 978 1 84835 245 2

Printed and bound in China

Author Vic Parker
Consultant Angela Royston
Project Editor Eve Marleau
Designer Kim Hall
Illustrator Mike Byrne

Publisher Steve Evans
Creative Director Zeta Davies
Managing Editor Amanda Askew

Picture credits
(t=top, b=bottom, l=left, r=right, c=centre,
fc=front cover)

Alamy 8t Keith Leighton
Corbis 19t Scott Sinklier
Dreamstime 19br Andy St John
Getty Images 19bl Stone/PBJ Pictures, 13b
Dorling Kindersley
Photolibrary 13t Age Fotostock/Frank Lukasseck
Shutterstock 4tl Tomo Jesenicnik, 4tc Jim Parkin,
4tr PetrP, 4bl PetrP, 4br Anbk, 5 Alessio Ponti,
6l Jim Parkin, 6r Microgen, 6–7 Martine Oger,
7tl PetrP, 7tr Tomo Jesenicnik, 7cr PetrP,
7bl Fotohunter, 7br Anbk, 8bl V J Matthew,
8bc Gelpi, 8br Joe Gough, 9t Matka Wariatka,
9cl Russ Witherington, 9ccl Denise Kappa,
9cr Richard Griffin, 9cr Viktor1, 9bl Ukrphoto,
9br Fanfo, 10 Thomas M Perkins, 11l Robert Milek,
11r Konstantin Remizov, 12tl Anbk, 12cl Stanislav
Komogorov, 12bl Mosista Pambudi, 12r Mosista
Pambudi, 13c Digital Shuts, 14tl Tomo Jesenicnik,
14cl Bruce Works, 14bl Orientaly, 14r Alexander
Briel Perez, 15t Sarah Johnson, 15c Dusan Po,
15bl Ints Vikmanis, 15br Rozaliya, 18tl Jim Parkin,
18cl David Hughes, 18bl N. Mitchell, 18r Noam
Armonn, 19c Woudew, 21l Hallgerd, 21r Hallgerd

Words in **bold** are
explained in the
glossary on page 22.

Contents

What are cereals?

Cereals are grains **from plants.
More cereal plants are grown
than any other type of** crop.

There are many different kinds of
cereal, such as barley, oats, wheat,
maize and rice.

Wheat

Maize

Barley

Oats

Rice

4

Grow a... wheat plant

1 Put the wheat grains into your jam jar.

2 Pour enough water in the jar to cover the grains. Put the thin cloth over the jar and secure it with an elastic band.

3 Put the jar in a warm place. Rinse and drain the grains twice a day.

4 In just a few days, your grains will start to sprout.

Cereal plants grow from seeds. They shoot up as straight, tall grasses. Wheat is grown in more parts of the world than any other cereal.

⇧ Cereal grains grow at the top in clusters, or groups, called ears.

Where are cereals grown?

Different types of cereal are grown all over the world.

They need the right conditions in order to grow. Some cereals need lots of rain. Other cereals need the soil to be quite dry.

North America

South America

Maize plants grow well in warm weather and damp soil. The United States of America produces nearly half of the world's maize.

Quinoa (say Keen-wah) grows well in the mountains of Peru in South America.

Oat plants grow well in cool **climates** with damp soil. Russia grows a lot of oats.

Wheat plants grow well in mild, damp weather. A lot of wheat is grown in China.

Europe

Asia

Barley is grown in cool places, such as Eastern Europe.

Africa

Oceania

Sorghum is grown in hot, dry places, such as Africa.

Rice grows well in hot places that have lots of rain. Most of the world's rice is grown in Asia.

How do we eat cereals?

We can eat cereals at any time of the day.

For lunch, you might have couscous with red peppers.

For dinner, you could have rice with a chicken curry.

In the morning, you might eat a breakfast cereal.

You will need

- 50 g wheatgerm
- 150 ml apple juice
- 2 bananas
- 500 g frozen berries
- Blender
- Glasses

Make a... wheatgerm smoothie

1 Put all the ingredients in a blender.

2 Blend for two minutes.

3 Pour into glasses and serve.

Pastry

Biscuit

Bread

Pasta

Doughnut

Pizza

We eat many foods made from flour, such as bread, pasta, pastry and biscuits. Flour usually comes from wheat, but other cereals can be made into flour, too, such as rice and maize.

9

Why does your body need cereals?

Cereals are carbohydrates. **They give your body energy and should make up a third of all the food we eat.**

Maize and other cereals contain **protein**, which your body needs to grow.

Bread made from wheat contains vitamin B, which your body needs to stay healthy.

Cereals such as oats and barley contain soluble **fibre**, which keeps your blood system healthy.

A grain of cereal is made up of three parts.

1 An outer layer called bran, which is fibre.

2 A larger part inside called the endosperm, which is mainly carbohydrate.

3 A small part inside called the germ, which is rich in protein.

Food news

Sometimes, just the endosperm in grain is used to make foods such as white bread. Other times, the whole grain is used to make foods such as brown bread.

Brown bread

White bread

Rice

How is rice grown?

Most rice farmers in Asia grow their seeds in patches of soil called seedbeds.

1 When the seeds sprout in the seedbeds in spring, the farmers replant them in bigger fields.

These fields are called paddies. They are naturally wet areas or are flooded with water. Rice needs plenty of water to grow.

2

3 The plants grow for three to five months. Then they are ready for **harvesting** in late autumn.

4 Some farmers harvest their rice by cutting the plant stems. The stems are tied in bundles and left to dry.

The plant stems are beaten against bamboo to separate the grains. Other farmers use machines for harvesting.

5

You will need

- 100 g puffed rice cereal
- 100 g golden syrup
- 60 g plain chocolate
- 75 g butter
- Saucepan
- Greased baking tin
- Wooden spoon

Make a... puffed rice treat

1 Put the golden syrup, plain chocolate and butter into the saucepan. Ask an adult to heat them until the chocolate has melted.

2 Take the saucepan off the hob and add the puffed rice cereal.

3 Stir well until all the cereal is coated in the mixture.

4 Pour the mixture into the greased tin and leave to cool. Put it in the fridge to harden.

Wheat

How is wheat grown?

Wheat needs plenty of rain to grow. Farmers sow wheat seeds in late autumn.

1 During winter, wheat plants grow slowly and look like a field of grass.

In spring, the wheat plants start to grow faster.

2

3 In summer, farmers use combine harvesters to pull the ears from the stems and separate the grains.

14

4 The grains are then turned into foods such as breakfast cereals and flour.

The wheat stalks die and dry out. This is called straw. It is then tidied into bundles.

5

6 The straw can be used for animal feed and bedding.

Food news

Wheat is grown in 42 out of 50 states in the United States of America.

Make bread

A lot of the flour that is made from wheat is turned into bread. Use this easy recipe to make your own bread.

You will need

- 125 g strong, plain wholemeal flour
- 100 g plain flour
- 1 tsp salt
- 1 tsp sugar
- 1 tbsp margarine
- 1 sachet (6 g) easy blend dried yeast
- 150 ml warm water
- Mixing bowl
- Wooden spoon
- Greased baking tray
- Piece of greased or oiled clingfilm

1

Put the flour, sugar, salt and margarine into a bowl and mix together.

2

Add the yeast and water and stir well. Use your hands to make the dough into a ball.

16

3 Push and stretch your dough for about 10 minutes until it feels soft and smooth. This is called kneading.

Put the dough onto the baking tray. Cover the tray with the greased clingfilm and put it in a warm place.

4

Ask an adult to set the oven to 230°C/450°F/Gas 8. Leave the dough for 30 minutes – it should double in size.

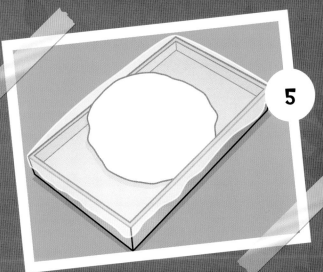

5

Remove the clingfilm and ask an adult to put the tray into the oven. Bake for 25 minutes until it is golden brown.

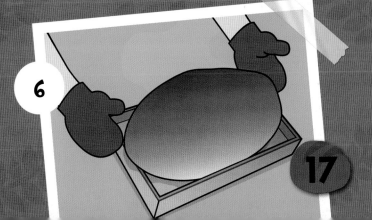

6

Maize

How is maize grown?

There are many different kinds of maize. Sweetcorn is one variety.

1 Farmers sow sweetcorn seeds in the spring.

Young shoots soon grow into tall stalks. The stalks develop ears, or cobs, of sweetcorn.

2

3 Long, silky threads grow out of the sweetcorn cobs, which eventually turn brown.

4 It takes about 2.5 months for sweetcorn to become ready for harvesting.

A machine called a combine harvester pulls the entire ears off the stems and separates the grains.

5

6 Some maize is taken to factories, where it is tinned or frozen. Ears of sweetcorn are also sent to shops for sale.

Eat a... baby corn

You can eat baby sweetcorn raw in a salad or add it to a vegetable stir-fry.

Make vegetable fried rice

Try using rice to make a healthy and tasty dish.

You will need

- 4 tbsp of rice
- 2 tbsp vegetable oil
- 1 red pepper, chopped
- 10 baby corn
- 6 mushrooms, chopped
- Salt and pepper
- Saucepan
- Frying pan
- Colander
- Water

1

Put the rice in the colander. Wash the rice four times.

Ask an adult to put the rice in a saucepan and cover with water. Cook at a low heat for about ten minutes.

2

3 Ask an adult to help you fry the vegetables in a frying pan with a little oil for five minutes.

Add the cooked rice and salt and pepper to the frying pan. Stir and serve straight away.

4

Food news

There are more than 40,000 types of rice grown all over the world.

Wild rice

Basmati rice

Glossary

Carbohydrates
Foods that contain sugar and starch, which gives us energy.

Climate
The typical weather of a certain area.

Crop
A plant grown in large amounts to be eaten or used by people or animals.

Fibre
A part of plants that our body can't digest. As fibre moves through our body, it soaks up water and makes it easier for us to get rid of waste food.

Grains
The tiny, dry fruits of a cereal plant.

Harvest
To gather, or collect, crops from the field.

Muslin
A very fine cotton fabric.

Protein
A substance found in food that our body needs to grow and repair itself.

Notes for parents and teachers

- Choose a variety of food. Talk about which foods are made from cereals, and which cereals the foods contain.

- Use the Internet to research where different cereals are grown and which conditions they need. Look at a map or globe to pick out the places where each cereal is grown.

- Find photographs of what different cereals look like when they are growing. Choose one for the children to draw and then label the different parts of the plant (roots, stem, branches, leaves, fruit). Talk about why our bodies need cereals to stay healthy and how much we should eat every day.

- Discuss the difference between refined and wholegrain cereals and explain why wholegrain cereals are best for us. Make a picture list of how we might make wholegrain choices instead of refined cereals. For example, choose a brown bread sandwich instead of a white bread sandwich.

- Talk about how we might use different types of cereal in cooking. Make an international cereal cookbook, with recipes and pictures from around the world and recipes for the children to try.

Index